Let's start by getting your mind in the thought process of taking care of problems and creating solutions. The more problems we correct and implement, the more patients we can help, and as a result the more money we can make. It has become common place to hear more and more about taking care of problems. Like many things we hear about, we don't take this simple concept literally. If there is a problem, finding a solution will attract the attention you need. Think about the company My Pillow. This company was started in the state of Minnesota with the idea of sleeping better. You see commercials and advertisements all of the time. When I wrote this, Michael Lindell the owner of My Pillow had recently launched a new line of luxury sheets, travel pillows, and many other small improvements on things we use to sleep better. Once Michael created one product the flood gates open. It all started with creating a solution to sleeping better. Best Buy and Target Corporation are also headquartered in Minnesota. It does not matter where you live, just create a solution to a problem.

You want to start this journey fast but efficient with quality care at the forefront. It has been stated many times that you only get one chance at starting a foundation. This is true, and why you have decided to start a clinic. The purpose of your clinic may be Dental, Chiropractic, Erectile Dysfunction, Weight Loss or many others. I have created a quick start guide based upon opening nearly 2 dozen clinics at the time of this writing. In my years I have been blessed to consult with many other industries to help build their businesses. I have even owned three furniture stores in the process. Each business in a unique venture, but the purpose and reason are the same. To help people. In the case of a clinic, often helping with pain of some type is why you chose this field or practice.

Here is a quick thought to ponder. Most people sit on an idea and continue to ponder ideas hoping to get started. This simple lack of fortitude is one of many ways we talk ourselves out of doing something great. It's difficult to think about something bigger than ourselves. As people of the internet we are becoming more and more about instant gratification. This guide is about getting the clinic up and running quickly so you can build that bigger picture. Stop sitting on the sidelines and watching others make ideas that you can make happen. Thinking bigger and more efficient. Many people talk about thinking bigger as the key. I agree with this 100%, and if you add think a little bit more efficient into the equation, now you have something special. Napoleon Hill said, "It Pays to Know How to Purchase Knowledge" This sets a foundation for everything we are going to cover. Here is one of the companies I have built based upon this very this principle. http://businessbuildersconsulting.com

I understand you may be worried what your friends say or what your family may think. For this reason, we are looking to hit the ground running with a single purpose in mind. Get the business running, then profitable, sustainable and finally running smoothly. This business will need your specific style and approach to be successful. Your added touch and care will be the reason this business is successful. This is a mission that is very much attainable. We all just need a little direction and guidance to get us started. Will there be problems along the way? Yes, that is why it is a business not a job or so-called career. Will you question yourself many times over? Yes, you will need to constantly be on top of your game to accomplish the mission. You will need to be detailed and as we complete goals one at a time. We don't have time to make excuses. If you need excuses, then just go to any blog talking about excuses then get it out of your system. Missteps will happen, but lack of effort will not be the problem.

I believe the next concept with complete faith. Hustle wins when talent is just not enough. If you outwork your competition, then ultimately you will choose to be successful. You can hire and add technology along the way. Adding a specialist is a way to even the playing field later. The only true advantage is effort. Yes, there knowing people and having connections, but you are reading this not calling that connection. Onward and upward we go!

There are many angles that you can take in business, and even more ideas that can work. I am not looking at something that can work. I want to teach you a simple model that once was just a philosophy. It has become a step by step guide to do exactly what has worked and what will work for you. Most people are not mission orientated enough to stay on top of the necessary tasks to start a business. Most also don't have the necessary resources to get everything accomplished. I am not saying that is bad, but if you just spent 8 plus years in school, you are not looking to start a Franchise. You are looking to make your place in the world. If you are reading this, we are at the point that you want to go on your own. Therefore, I have created this process in the spirit of letting people know this can happen. This is a short read on purpose. I do not want to spend a bunch of time boring you with details that will be learned along the way, but give you tips while you are working to attain the goal. The goal is real. I am going to teach you how to build a business.
This is your business Are you ready?

I am a firm believer in the concept of a mastermind group. Surround yourself with people that are smarter than yourself. As of this book written in 2020 there is more outsourcing than ever before. Here is an example of this method even a century ago. Thomas Edison had 3 months of schooling but is known as one of the greatest inventors in history. Not because he had knowledge learned in the classroom, but because he was smart enough to surround himself with men and women that were educated, and experienced in businesses that he wanted to be in. Another example of this: Henry Ford went to the Dodge Brothers to create a motor for him, hired engineers to put his ideas into production. He was the driving force behind the assembly line that revolutionized the world as we know it. Henry Ford had approximately 8 years of schooling in one classroom. I am not saying this to put a bad light on college or training, but to help you understand that a good business model is a great start. We all need help at one time or another.

I am not concerned how book smart you are or what your schooling grade says you are. I am wanting to talk to people that have driven and ambitious qualities. This same person wants something bigger than themselves and understands that more than 8 out of 10 business will fail to ever become profitable inside of 3 years. This is the reason people franchise. You are reading this because you want to explore a different angle. We will help you get started and allow you to spread your wings. I don't want you getting stuck in a model that you don't feel comfortable with. When changes need to be made to make the company yours, then do it. Our goal is to get you going, train you how to become profitable, and let you fly.

There may be 100 question that can be thinking right now. Are you looking at the right industry to get in? Is this the right time to get started in a certain industry? Is my city large enough? Is there too much competition or saturated? These questions and many are very important and are asked by the most successful businesses. Are you a salesperson or more of an engineering mind? Can I hire the right people to do this for me? What will be the most important task I can do every day to keep my business profitable? Once these questions are answered you can proceed with certainty. We will walk with you step by step to teach you the small starting points that need to be addressed.

I once hired an Ivy League Graduate. He was brilliant and used his intelligence to interview like a champion. I was impressed as he hit a home run on all stages of the interview process. My gut instinct told me that something was off, but I had to know as his interview was the best I have seen. He was prepared in every aspect of the interview and had all the leadership qualities I was looking for. I brought him in for 3 interviews instead of my normal 2-part process just to be sure. I hired him and the first few weeks were great. His leadership was solid, and I was thinking I need to look at this school more for hires.

I went to the clinic one day unannounced and he was showing the staff his car, house, and essentially bragging about himself. I pulled him aside and told him that the clinic seems to be getting behind, and if he knew why. His statement to me was simple: We needed to add more people to take on the amount of work. I explained to him that hundreds of clinics run under this model around the country and do just fine. I ended up letting him go and found out quickly that he did not have common sense to run his own life on a day to day basis. He made six figures annually and was always broke due to lack of self-control. He could not get out of his own way, so he always was worried about things that didn't matter instead of doing his job. Quickly people under his management started getting reckless. He showed lack of leadership to his staff by worrying about personal things at work like credit card payments and ordering personal things on Amazon. I ended up moving on from a well-educated interviewee because of this. At the end of the day Lesson learned. I did not ask enough questions. A resume and a smile are just that. I spent the next month fixing this problem myself. There was no one to blame but myself. I hired him.

The manager that replaced him made about 70% of his starting rate. The normal pay rate I started a manager at. We all make mistakes. The new manager was always focused at the office and dependable. I ended up promoting her and never looked back. Point of this is simple. If you want something you can attain it. Your ability to keep moving forward in hard times is a guiding force and is not written on a grading scale or a piece of paper. Keep moving forward and keep your focus the main thing. If I need highly educated people for a task or project, you can hire them or contract them to do the work. If I were to start another company who do I want in a manager? A person with drive, want, desire, and determination are the qualities I look for. Her ability to manage others is a must. Some people want success, and others make it happen through effort. Education is understanding the situation as much as anything. You can contract the specialist. Think carefully about the person you choose to run a clinic for you. Do they match the ideals that you covet? There is no such thing as the perfect employee or person. If they are as good as you, then you may have competition if you're not careful. In this guide we will get you plenty of the right people, just be very careful to fall in love with an employee. If they're good enough they may move on or just took the position as a stop gap.

Week 1 – Organizing and Ordering

Day 1.

a) By now you have an office and location secured and ready to move in. Deep breathe as this is happening. Let's be organized. You really don't need anything special today if you have a phone and laptop you can get to work at the office. Today people are just using phones to do everything. I happen to have two that I use, and your phone has a hotspot capability if you like the laptop. I like to work at the clinic the entire time during the set-up process. There are multiple reasons for this. 1. You will want to look around and determine where everything is going to be put. it's the place you will be ordering things for. A phone with data works just as well, you will not be able to print unless your printer a printer from home. Bring paper, pen, clear tape, black marker and a tape measure with you. As you are doing set up having a place to make notes and put them on the wall will be crucial for time management. This will allow visual steps to be taken and keep you on task.

b) Priority #1 stuff today. Determine the clinic name and secure domain for website and email addresses. If you have not done already is to get FEIN number. Many times, this can take 2 weeks. Let's get the important things taken care of day 1. Once this is done, we can look for business insurance. I have found when starting an email that Google is user friendly choice. Most future

employees will know the Google format. Everybody has a Gmail account. The extras that Google does like the Google Calendar, Drive, Hangouts, and others will be necessary later in the business development and staff training. No need to reinvent the wheel at this stage. If you're and IT person and training is simple for you go for it. I just stress the fact that people have different learning curves. Something to think about.

c) Determine pay scale you will have for staff. I am a big fan of the person reading this to do sales and the call position to start. If you are not comfortable then have someone you know will take care of your business in the same manner you will. This is a big position. You're the driving force and need to know this specific process. 40K annual salary plus incentives will find you a good salesperson when the time is right. The Call Person position is between $13 - $18 per hour and I prefer paying $5-10 per show. You want your patients to show up. Appointments are great, but appointments showing up is the name of the game. Medical technician is $17 to $22 per hour depending on market size. A salary based on this price range works as well. I have done fine both ways, just a preference. One of each position to start day one. Insurance is an option for employees, but not necessary to start. Your staff will be excited to help build a company from the ground up. This is an excellent experience for any person to be a part of. This is your value add in place of insurance. Once you are running 6 months. Then start looking.

d) I can show you full details of what the advertisements should say word for word if you want. Please note: Do not put your phone number in the advertisement. This is a bad idea and will cause you a lot of headaches with time wasting people. In your advertisement tell them that they must include a paragraph about why they want the position and how they may fit your organization. You must include this in a Word or PDF resume. If they do not follow your instructions, that will give you incite as to how much they pay attention, and if they can follow instructions later. Your clinic will be small. Every person needs to show the ability to follow your leadership. Start it now!

e) Run ads to start the interview process for the call person, sale position and medical technician job immediately. I like Indeed and Craigslist. Craigslist gets a quick response and Indeed brings more quality in my experience, but I have done well from both. Remember we are looking at starting off on an expedited time frame. Time is money, and so is good quality, but often you don't know who you are hiring until the business is running. We take many steps to be as sure as we can, but there is no true perfect answer. Starting in your network of people I a wise choice. You may know a person or two that make sense for you. This will lessen the curve initially. If you are the physician, then you may know a good medic candidate. This person can be an EMT, Paramedic, CNA, Nurse or equivalent. Some states may vary. Check locally.

Note: Do not put a phone number in the advertisement. This is can cause a lot of unnecessary work later.

If you have not done a website yet chose the format for option #1:

*** Medical Technician --- Medical Office $18 Per Hour ***

($18 per Hour) All Daytime Hours working with a Licensed Medical Doctor

Full Time medical professional needed for unique specialty medical clinic. We help Men with Erectile Dysfunction and weight loss. Please understand we work with lots of geriatric patients. This is a great position for a Medical Assistant, EMT, Paramedic and/or Nurse. Must be 100% dependable, have a positive personality, good work habits including, but not limited to enthusiasm and desire. Due to the unique nature of our medical practice we work with mostly male patients. We want our staff and patients to be comfortable with the work environment. Daytime Hours, no evenings, or weekends. Email resume with a brief note about yourself and salary history in a Word or PDF document. We promote from within. Beautiful medical building in (your city). Great staff to work with. Please note there will be a raise to $18.50 per hour after successful 3 months from start date. Important to be flexible. Please Thank You Management!

The 2nd option: Only if your website is ready to be viewed or very close

*** APPOINTMENT & CARE PROFESSIONAL --- Medical Office ***

Incoming calls and call backs (40K first year can earn $50K or more)

FULL-TIME telephone care professional needed for unique specialty medical clinic, take inbound calls from advertising we do in many media's, follow script and book appointments. High quality advertising done in house. You ABSOLUTELY MUST have at least (5) years' experience working on the telephone or inbound sales to be considered, be 100% dependable, have a positive personality, good work habits are a must. Due to the unique nature of our medical practice we request well-groomed applicants, thank you for understanding. Daytime Hours, no evenings, or weekends. $18 per hour plus patient care bonuses paid bi-weekly. Email resume with a brief note about yourself, and why you would be a good fit. Please send in Word or PDF document only. Beautiful medical building. Great staff to work with and we promote from within. Our website is *********@****.com please check out our state-of-the-art website :)

f) Posting an advertisement bulletin at the local hospital is effective and inexpensive option. People like to change jobs, don't forget recent graduates are changing jobs they don't like more than ever. I read that in the first couple of years out of college it's not uncommon to have 4 jobs per year. Doing these steps on the first day will pays dividends later. Run ads for sales on a separate time than medical technicians in the interview process. Again, this depends on the positions you will be assuming to begin with.

Note on interviewing: Some people like group interviews and then one on one. I prefer grouping 5 people at a time to make your time valuable. If a person is turned off knowing they will still get one on one time, then they probably are not the right person anyway. Thought to ponder on this: I like to see how people react around other candidates that are peers in a position. Add a picture of the building they will be working in. This adds instant validity to the position. There are a few ways to add credibility. If your clinic is new, then focus on the employee's ability to start something new and the gorgeous building you are located in. Highlight local attractions or monuments that may be near, like the mall or popular fast food.

g) This option is assuming that you are not the physician who will be running the clinic. Only if you need staffing from aa physician.

Call Locum Tenens Company of choice (this is a physician placing company), and get the Doctor, Physician's Assistant or Nurse Practitioner. Each state has different rules, so let the tenens company know you want a nice picture of physician's license for the wall to display it. Also, know the hours we will need the doctor(s) This will be of major concern to the physician, and the company you task for helping. I can give a few very solid companies. Be aware good ones don't charge you until they get you someone. They also don't require crazy lengthy contracts. This is 2020 people. We are about results. These companies are out there and constantly helping with staffing. There in dozens of options online.

Day 1 is complete. Take a couple pictures of your clinic, this will give you a nice head start for tomorrow.

Day 2.

a) Choose Software to run the office. Practice Fusion is free with soap notes & scheduling in one. You can always add a more advanced system later. It is great as most medical people will be familiar and the software is user friendly. Do we need any furniture, desks or filing cabinets? All of this can be bought at Staples, online or any box store you prefer. Some people like used, but office furniture is nice and inexpensive at Staples/ Office Depot or a similar type of outfit of your choice. Let's go through some important questions to start off Day 2. How many stand-alone professional office guest chairs do we need? These are the chairs sitting in the waiting room; 8 maybe 10? How many Rolling chairs for the staff?

b) If not something you have already taken care of: Start the process of setting up a website. It must be very professional looking. There are many good options here. I recommend using WordPress _if you are doing it yourself_, as they are the leader for indexing your website. They are Google and user friendly. 2nd Choice here is just hire a professional. $1200 or so for a sharp looking and functional website. Time is money. I would just pay the professional and not worry about it. This can be done in a week and be ready for you by the start of week 2.

c) Start the process with advertising companies (Lot's to do here) advertising can be a tricky business, but the simple way to not get overwhelmed is hire experts. I can give you good options if you want advice. I don't want to endorse anyone in this guide without making other advertising companies mad at me. I have a business partner that does this for a living. The only thing to be sure of is to ask if they track calls and give reports. How often do they? Is there extra cost and how long are the contracts if any?

How long have they been in business?

d) Get High Speed Internet process started and phone options. Xfinity is a simple low cost and user-friendly solution. Get a <u>Hunt Group</u> so you can manage the phone system and track everything on a mobile basis. It's your company. You need to be in the know about everything that is happening. If calls are being missed it is costing you money. Ask the question about installing wall jacks? This is so you can hook up your credit card machine, television or other amenities.

e) Remember the pictures you took yesterday, now is time to write on your paper places for phones, phone jacks, TV's and other cables that may need to be installed. Write with a black marker and clear tape them to the places that need to be done.

f) Get finance companies selected and set up training for following weeks. There are many good finance companies, just make sure the finance company is paying your practice not the patient. Go online and look for medical company financing or some variation of. It will only take a week to set this up. You will need the Clinic name and EIN eventually. First things first though. Time to find one you like and get the process started.

g) Signage. We now have the walls taped with places that wires and TV's are going, so now we need to get the signage for the front door, inside and on the marquee of we have one. Is there signage by the elevator? Do we have it outside? Small things that need to be done now so we don't run into issues later. Tomorrow we will get into some serious ordering. For now, let's just take a step back and think about the amazing journey we started

Day 3

a) Order exam tables (do we need 2, 3 or 4) I like the stirrups and steps with storage. Maximizes space and professionalism. There are many places like Craigslist and online that will sell you very nice equipment. Both new

and used are options. You can be picky. There are many dozens of good companies.

b) Order Anatomical Posters and matching frames (3 or 4 kinds), just find the closest anatomy posters to your business. Chiropractic, Weight Loss, Dental. These all have sectors online, but there are many companies that do a great job of this as a stand-alone company. Type online and search away.

c) Order posters for the walls, tri fold brochures, and a laminated bullet point sheet that nicely explains your services. Time to order business cards if you already have the phone number ready from the phone company. People love to hold onto something with substance. (Use local Print shop) order a minimum of 500 Generic business cards for the clinic. No staff names just clinic or physicians name is fine. Until you have the right staff this can be a hassle otherwise. Always amazed by people that start a job and quit in a month. This is your company not your employees. You are already letting them be a part of the opening. Focus on the main thing. This is not the time to be cute.

d) that you did signs with. By waiting a day, you can add onto your order and generally get a bulk discount □

e) Get Magazines to put in office that will make sense for your patients. Simply put: No food magazines in a weight loss clinic.

f) Wall posters that look good in the office. Get professional and simple with normal colors. No need to get exotic.
People like normalcy. A nice picture of the city is always a winner.

g) If you have nice built in sinks with plenty of cabinets you will be fine, but if the rooms are large you may want plastic folding tables (sturdy and white) 4, 6 or 8 foot depending on space size. I like staples. Maybe an extra cabinet. You can always add on later.

h) Pictures frames for doctor's license. Match the larger frames you ordered before. Amazon, Walmart, Target, or any online store is simple and efficient.

i) Order Credit Card Processing machine at same time as setting up bank account. This needs to be done today or by the end of week 1. You don't want shipping issues on your credit card processing system. Use your banks system for convenience.

Last - Check your resumes on Craigslist, Indeed, and any other sites you posted. Set up phone interviews for day 5. Set up 3 times 10:00, 2:00 and 6:00 for phone interviews. Do these 15 minutes apart. Keep detailed notes on each person. Print or save their resume with notes about them and who they are. Be sure to make notes of their comments. Both good and bad. Everybody gets busy, these notes will save you later when you forget the conversation.

I know this may seem weird, but you are going to be busy, and it is very easy to forget who you are talking to. You will oversee 100 tasks to get the business started. It's my preference to send them an email to set up a time. I never leave my phone number as I need people who are interested and serious about getting started. If you leave your phone number people will catch you off guard. 1st impressions are important.

2nd, you will get a lot of time wasters.

Day 4

Order Flags for exam rooms. This allows for proper set up and keeps your staff aware of what patients are in the room. Set up Flag system protocols (get 3, 4 or 5) depending on the clinic size. For some reason these are slow. That is why we are ordering today.

Reminder to buy 4 Phones for the office and set up internet (did you already get them when you went with Xfinity or some other carrier? This is more of a follow up than anything else. You will need a phone.

Buy Computers from Staples or store of your preference. Get 3 for sure. I prefer to always get the same model. Allows for cross training.

Order your preference of an All in one Printer, copier, scan and fax. Then order an inexpensive black and white printer so you can keep costs down, but still have all options to be professional. Order spare toners cartridge for Printer(s) Longer lasting are usually well worth it.

Order 2 tablets for patient info and growth as you will want to become digital in a few months. This is a necessary growth model. Not just a fast start option.

Time to order supplies

I am just going to simply put a list of things together you will need. There may be a few things you don't need or a few extras, but this is 90% of what you will need regardless of clinic type you are going to start. If you are not fully organized, then things will get missed. Best time to take care of a problem is before it happens. Let's prepare to be the best and fake it until we are.

Trifold Brochure holder (staples)

Printer paper. Professional grade (1 case)

Envelopes use VIP large 6 x 9 (100) and normal letter size (500) (white only)

Pens (blue or black) (3 boxes of 12)

Wall clock for main office. (none in exam rooms ever)

Wall flags for each exam room (protocols will need to be set up later)

Door Pockets also called wall hangers (12) Comes in packs of 4

Order power strips and extension cords based upon projected needs

Yellow or variety color markers

Black Markers sharpie

Pen holders (3, 4 or 5)

Paper clip holders (unless you don't use them)

Tape dispensers (4)

Scotch tape (comes in pack of 12)

Staplers (4)

Cash box (small for bills and checks) You can get these at Staples, Amazon, Walmart, Target and many more.

Folder bins to hang on the wall so we have a file folder for each exam room in a separate organized way. (3 or 4, or 5)

Paper bins (PLASTIC) that are stackable (4 sets) (each has 4 or 5) (Amazon, Staples) Great for paper files and organizing.

Manilla Folders (100) & Folder hangers (100)

Paper Towels (2 cases)

Pillows (4) and Pillowcases (100 in a case) from Amazon or similar Get a firm pillow. You don't want your patient sinking in and feeling uncomfortable. Unless you don't use exam tables, they you may not need pillows.

Clipboards (12 pack) get nice looking to match your style

Credit card processor paper (comes in rolls of 9) (Staples, Amazon)

Calculators (3 or 4 big button Calculators)

Sticky notes

Scissors (3 or 4)

Business card holders (3)

Rubber Gloves Large 6 boxes and 4 XL gloves. Use blue or neutral colors. Don't get crazy colors. It can cause issues amongst staff.

Hand sanitizer for each room. (12 to start)

Generic Tissue Paper for each room. (get a case, comes in 30) Ultrasound Gel if you are using a Doppler. (get a case)

Cuffs for blood pressure. (large digital and X large manual)

Stethoscope even if medical technicians and doctor have one.

Cavicide wipes or spray bottle. Get a case to clean tables and 4 bottles of Alcohol. (amazon or others)

Exam table paper comes in 12 per pack. Get 18" not 21" size. Most tables only have holders for 18" rolls.

Cotton balls (1 pack)

Glass Jars for the clinic (12) for cotton balls, finger cots, aesthetics or anything that applies to your business. They look professional.

Stamps for mailing. (roll of 50 or 100)

Paper Shredder (must shred 8 pages at a time)

Weight Scale at Amazon for patients. Get a specialty model that checks the whole-body composition. Very Important!

Keurig, coffee with sugar and cream for patients and staff.

Do we need a fridge or Microwave? Any other appliances? Now is the time to monitor this and get it under control.

Check your resumes on Craigslist, Indeed, and any other sites you posted set up phone interviews for day 5. Set up 3 times 10:00, 2:00 and 6:00 for phone interviews. Do these 15 minutes apart. Keep detailed notes on each person, and print or save their resume with notes about them and who they are. Be sure to make notes of their comments. Both good and bad.

What is going on with the Locum Tenens Process? Check on this.

Questions and thoughts

Do we have bottled water, or do we have the water machine?

Where is the bathroom. Is it close to the elevator? Easy for patients?

What door will the patients be using? Where will signage go?

Care of our patients is a big reason we are starting this, so do we need to add any cabinets or a new piece of Granite?

Hours of operation and where do you place it? Do you want to buy a nice-looking wall poster for it or a standalone on the counter?

Any other machines or tools we need that are mission critical?

Follow up to check with the company who is installing other devices like cable television or wireless, phones to make sure it's done.

Who is going to be around to get deliveries from orders like Amazon?

Do you hang a sign when you are gone so that the delivery guy does not miss you? This is a simple sign that has your phone number or allows the delivery person to put the box in front of your door. Your choice,

Day 5

Today is an organization day. I gave you a lot to do in days one through four. Look around. There has been a lot accomplished so far.

Now is a day to go back and check on orders, loose ends with shipping, furniture, and supplies. Is there a vendor that is delayed or that does not fit with your time? Now is the day to make the adjustments. You should have some resumes and people interested in doing interviews on the phone. We were on top of it and took care of this, but today is the day to do phone interviews. Have the entire job description in front of you. I prefer printing it off as I want to be as detailed as possible. I have separate notes for each person.

These are employees that will oversee your company. Put your cell phone on silent and start calling people that you set up on day 3 and day 4. Set these interviews up in person for 2 times Tuesday, Wednesday, and Thursday and Friday of week 2. 10:00 AM and 6:00 PM seem to work well. Remember only 5 people max at a time. Keep it small so you can do 15 minute 1 on 1 interviews. That way it will be done in 75 minutes. It's very efficient and lets them know you respect their time as well. Order of the interview is by who showed up first. Simple honor system.

Take good notes in the interview process. If you do a lot of interviews, then how do you remember the person you were interviewing? Do you take pics or highlight something? Who is candidate # 1, 2, 3 and why? What stood out most? Did they have a pleasant voice? Let them know they are interviewing with the person that makes the final hiring decision, and that if you bring them in for an interview, they will be considered a serious candidate. Make them aware you appreciate their time, and you expect the same. Keep the interview on the phone short with facts about the position. Let them know this will be a great position for people who are self-starters and want to be in a position of authority. Must be well groomed and on time. You expect them to come to work every day and can count on them to do their job. Lastly, I like to tell them that this is a rare opportunity so help start a medical clinic. I like to hear the enthusiasm.

BE SURE HIRING PAPERWORK IS READY FOR INTERVIEWS NEXT WEEK. PRINT OFF ONLINE. MAKE SURE THE RESUME YOU USE STATES EQUAL OPPORTUNITY EMPLOYER AND THAT WE DO BACKGROUND CHECKS. THIS IS A MUST EVERYTIME.

Congratulations you made it through week #1. A lot of the heavy lifting is done.

Week 2

Interviewing and hiring are the focus this week, after that we are just finishing up from week one. A lot of the time, we will have potential staff help us set up, so they feel ownership, and get comfortable. This helps take care of many questions in the process and allows the interview to be more than just sitting. I will touch a little later doing a mobile interview in the 2-Part interview. It will allow you to check out posture, and important things like how quick they can attend to a task, follow instructions and think on their feet. All the things that will be needed when you bring them aboard. A sitting interview does very little to qualify. This will be discussed further on day 2.

Day 1

Hang up posters in the clinic, wall art and making the place feel like a clinic. This does not need to be completed in any way, but acceptable to do interviews. People love the idea of a new clinic, utilize it to your advantage.

Set up computers, and printers if they have come in. Set up a place to do interviews. Make Sure you have 6 chairs set up nicely. One for you and the other 5 for potential employees. Remember these are the chairs you bought to set up in the sitting area. Double check to be sure all new hire forms are printed and that you have enough. Tomorrow is the start of the interview process. Clipboards should be here by now. Have the clipboards preloaded with hiring forms, then put them on each chair. This shows you have it together to the potential employee. Set up a one on one interview area with executive chairs. This is in one of the exam rooms preferably.

Call persons and salespersons generally do not need to give 2 weeks' notice, because employers let them go immediately. Medical technicians often do. So, this is important to understand when doing interviews. I like to do a 2-part interview. Part 1 is a sit down and talk about the position interview. Part-2 is the interviewee walking around with me as I show them what is expected. Maybe meet other staff if I have any and explain that this is a fast-paced office. If I am very interested in an interviewee, I will do a 2nd interview outside of normal times, but I generally like to keep the format in place. The times we set up for interviews are generally easy to work with. Four days and 2 slots are more than enough if a person is interested. They can do it before, after or during work. People will find a way to interview when they see something they like.

Don't assume otherwise.

Day 2, 3, 4, 5

In Person interviews today and every day. Dress professional. Have a nice area set up for interviews. Be mindful that there will be deliveries this week and that the interviewee candidates should be made aware of this during the group interview. Remember the best time to take care of a problem is before it happens. If candidates are aware, then it is expected and just part of the awesome process you are setting up. It is your job to set the expectations. Tell them the truth, you are looking for the right person and will do what needs to be done until you find the right person(s).

Remember this interview process is about the mobile concept. Let them know your phone may ring and you may need to take it. You expect to have a busy clinic. These people need to know you are not looking for a lazy person. You will want high energy people with a positive attitude This needs to be shown by you as a leader for them to understand what you want. So, do it in the interview. Show them around after you went through their job history and explain how busy we can get. Tell them most employees pack a lunch. The sense of urgency can be exciting to the prospect. In the interview let them know you do a 2-part interview. You will want them back a 2nd time. If they won't then they made the decision for you. Some will do a 2nd interview this week and this can allow the 2 weeks' notice if needed.

Each day this week. Check on more resumes and the process of the potential physician if the Locum Tenens is working on this for you. I like to set up the Doctors in week 3 or interviews when we need one.

As you can see, we are focused on the important things, but not putting off the minutia that need to be attended to. These are keys to getting the clinic up and running in the time and manner we need to succeed.

a) Make sure the email and text messaging system through your medical software is set up this week. A must for

   good show rates. Patients showing up is a must in our business.

b) Directions and address info on desk by each phone. (detailed directions are a must) with phone number, fax number and call forwarding to voice mail if needed. (by every single phone) There is no excuse to not have the Doctors name and info on hand. Include EIN and all clinic info including Phone number.

c) Credit Card Procession machine test. Must be tested and set up the day it arrives so you don't forget. This our lifeblood. Must know it works and how to use it. Be sure to train staff when time is appropriate. This may be another week but know how to yourself so you can train others.

d) Find a place to get Lab Coates and scrubs. I like Logos and names of physician on Lab coat. Scrubs can have the logo and name as well, but if a technician quits after a week it can be a costly mistake.

Week 3

This is a hiring and training week. If you have not met and hired the physician yet, then this will be done this week. A lot of the time this can be done week two, but week three is generally the time this is done. Same process for interviews and hiring as week two. This week you will make more decisions on staff. I like to hire on Monday and Tuesday. A lot of time the call person will ready to go and the medical technician will start next week Monday or Tuesday. Having the extra time with your call person is good, as you will want to make sure she has the same enthusiasm as when you hired her.

If you are doing a weight loss business model, then you might not even need a Doctor or medical technician. So, in this case you will be looking for a fitness person. Oddly enough these same people are often medics or firemen. So just some food for thought when it comes to hiring for different business models in the medical field.

Have the employees learn the sales tracking/appointment scheduling software. This important so that anyone can answer the phone if needed. Cross training on many jobs will be important. Deliveries will still be coming in this week. Have someone there to receive orders. You get so busy that this is easy to forget. Same policy as the first 2 weeks.

1. Advertising to be started some-time this week. There're a few ways to start I like to start advertising 1 week before opening. Spend the necessary time with your advertising person to be sure this is perfect.

2. Where will mail be delivered? Do we need to set anything up?

3. Spend 2 separate one half days with Appointments Setter before phone rings live. Do not skip this step. Yes, it could be you doing the simulations. Check the Voicemail and answering systems.

4. Test credit card machine with a penny. Make sure receipts are correct and that the spelling is correct on your receipt. Professionalism is the name of the game.

5. Where is the bathroom located? Our patients will need this information readily. Knowledge of the area is important for each

employee to have. Patients like the professionalism and knowledge. I don't know is not an acceptable answer.

6. Who sits where in the office? Is there a glaring hiring need yet? I like to have the call person more in the back to they can answer without being bothered by patients. If you are doing sales, then you will want to greet anyway.

7. Do you have good back up candidates if your first staffer does not work? Remember earlier in the interview process you labeled candidate #1, 2, 3 etc. Now you know why.

8. Have all orders arrived that you made in week 1 or made week 2 if necessary?

9. Finalize business cards to be delivered. Probably had a few drafts done by now. Any final posters, printed materials, and signs in the clinic?

4th Week. Opening the clinic on a Thursday

Monday - full training and finalize set up. Recheck your list. Has everything showed up that you ordered? If there was stalls on ordering, what is the status and follow up?

Tuesday - finish training (full dress rehearsal day) and be sure staff knows what we expect in every step of the clinic. Paperwork, seating, answering phones etc.

Wednesday - Fill out clip boards, make sure all appointments have been confirmed and patients have good directions. Yes, people still care about directions and landmarks. Is there a leader that is emerging from the staffers? Are there any mannerisms or posture that need to be brought to their attention as staff members?

Thursday - Open clinic with all staff being there 1 hour early. Meeting to cover loose ends. You are the leader. Remember that staff will look to you... Game time! You are prepared!

Opening the clinic on a Thursday will allow you and the staff to get started while learning strengths and weaknesses together. At the end of these important 2 days, you will be able to determine necessary changes that may need to take place. The genius behind this is: You have the weekend to digest and adapt. Business can get overwhelming. Don't let this deter you. Then come Monday both you and your staff will have a better idea of the rigors or pain points that may exist. Sometimes a full week juts drains you. Utilize the mistakes that I have made over the years, and have some fun doing it.

I hope your business the very best. There are many more tips, and secrets, but I gave you an honest way to get a business off the ground. Just go to http://businessbuildersconsulting.com if you some guidance from one of my excellent colleagues and business partners. I leave you with this quote:

"In This Time of Constant Information Ignorance is a Choice"

Justin Webster

www.ingramcontent.com/pod-product-compliance
Lightning Source LLC
Chambersburg PA
CBHW031510210526
45463CB00008B/3171